The Rich Man
and the Shoe-maker

The Rich Man

A FABLE BY LA FONTAINE

Franklin Watts, Inc.

and the Shoe-maker

ILLUSTRATED BY BRIAN WILDSMITH

575 Lexington Avenue New York N.Y. 10022

Once upon a time there lived
a poor but cheerful shoe-maker.

He was so happy he sang all day long.
The children loved to stand round his
window to listen to him.

Next door to the shoe-maker lived a rich man.

He used to sit up all night to count his gold.

In the morning he went to bed, but he could not sleep

because of the sound of the shoe-maker's singing.

One day he thought of a way of stopping the singing.

He wrote a letter to the shoe-maker asking him to call.

The shoe-maker came at once, and to his surprise
the rich man gave him a bag of gold.

When he got home again, the shoe-maker opened the bag. He had never seen so much money before! He sat down at his bench and began, carefully, to count it. The children watched through the window.

There was so much there
that the shoe-maker was
afraid to let it out of his
sight. So he took it to bed
with him.

But he could not sleep for worrying about it. So he got out of bed and

went to hide it in the attic, but he
was not sure if that was a good place.

Very early in the morning he got up and
brought his gold down from the attic. He had
decided to hide it up the chimney instead.

But after breakfast he thought it
would be safer in the chicken-house.
So he hid it there.

But he was still uneasy and in a little while he dug
a hole in the garden, and buried his bag of gold in it.

It was no use trying to work. He was too
worried about the safety of his gold. And as
for singing, he was too miserable to utter a
note. He could not sleep, or work, or sing—
and, worst of all, the children no longer
came to see him.

At last the shoe-maker felt so unhappy that he seized his bag of gold and ran next door to the rich man. 'Please take back your gold,' he said. 'The worry of it is making me ill and I have lost all my friends. I would rather be a poor shoe-maker, as I was before.'

And so the shoe-maker was
happy again, and sang all day
at his work.

First published 1965 by Oxford University Press
First American publication 1966 by Franklin Watts, Inc.
575 Lexington Avenue, New York, N.Y. 10022
Fourth Impression 1970

SBN 531–01538–6

Library of Congress Catalog Card Number: 65–20551

PRINTED IN AUSTRIA